The Blue Bat Art Book

A catalogue record of this book is available from the British Library

First Edition: December 2020

ISBN: 978-1-84375-627-9

To order additional copies of this book please visit:
http://www.prestige-press.com/shirleyhughes

Published by: Prestige Press
Email: info@prestige-press.com
Web: http://www.prestige-press.com

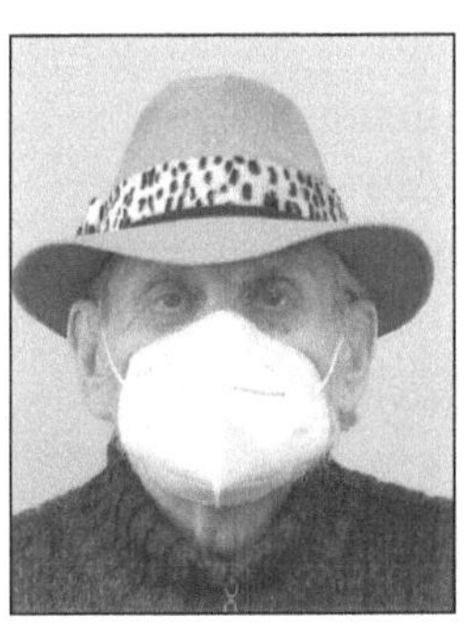

Cover Design by David L Hughes, resident artist in Lockdown.
This book is for him.

About the Cover Design
The Bue Bat, in the order of Chiroptera, illustrated on the front cover depicts, demonstrates and represents art, sculpture, design, colour, imagination and painting.

Other Books by the author:

Persona
In Depth Of Soul
The Choices of Being
The Grass Isn't Always Greener
Rose Tinted Glasses
Leah's Journey
The Pink Flamingo Fellowship
Bilé
Academia
Pathway To The Unconscious
Sartre – In Focus
Mooloo
The Symbolic Mask
Ghostopia
Recognising The Soul
Transformation
Philosophy of Friendship

The Blue Bat Art Book

by

Dr. Shirley Hughes

Prestige Press

Contents

Note

I am a philosopher and my husband an artist. Noting his passion and interest for his artistic endeavours and the time and effort he puts into every project including my book cover designs, set me thinking about the philosophical aspects of art and the questions they raise. It is a more complex topic than I could ever have imagined.

The characteristics and persona every artist seems to have and need is a burning desire to create, to be immersed in each and every piece of work.

Philosophers like myself have the intellect and a deep passion for words, writing and philosophy and the desire to reveal the answers to the questions raised by every chosen topic, this one being art.

Introduction

Influenced by its social, political, religious and economic environment, the purpose of art constantly changes. Art expresses and emphasises a vast diversity of emotions, beliefs and ideas such as beauty, hope, life, death, chaos and order. It can be decorative, philosophical, religious or simply entertaining, and whether it is meant to be enjoyed, to arouse imagination, trigger emotions or is carrying a message, it always chronicles or mirrors its age. Even when breaking established traditions all artists reflect their time and place in history. Art also helps us to recognise how humans have perceived themselves. Some form of art has been made by nearly all societies. It is not neat and ordered, and overlaps and changes, cross influences and reacts. It is never made in a vacuum, which is what can make it so confusing at times. Mainly focusing on Western artistic developments, this is an introduction to many of the most important movements, styles and developments in art from prehistory to the present day. It also looks philosophically at some of the most significant art produced by the most ground-breaking artists, and considers many artistic themes. Art explores and depicts a great variety of inventions, ideas, influences and artists themselves today, as it has done historically.

Chapter 1

Art As A Word

First we must recognise the obvious. Art is a word and words are also concepts, they are organic and change their meaning through time. In the olden days art meant crafts. It was something you could excel at through practice and hard work. You learnt how to paint and sculpt and you learnt the special symbolism of your era. Through Romanticism and the birth of individualism, art came to mean originality. To do something new and never heard of defined the artists. Their personality became essentially as important as the artwork itself. During the era of Modernism the search for originality led artists to re-evaluate art. What could art do? What could it represent? Could you paint movement? Could you paint Cubism, Futurism or non material abstract Expressionism? Fundamentally, could anything be regarded as art?

A way of trying to solve this problem was to look beyond the work itself and focus on the art world. Art was that which the institution of art, artists, critics and art historians were prepared to regard as art and which was made public through their institutions and galleries. That is Institutionalism made famous by and through the artist Marcel Duchamp's ready-mades. Institutionalism has been the prevailing notion through the later part of the 20th century at least in academia and it still holds a firm grip on our conceptions. One example is the Swedish artist Anna Odell.

Her film sequence 'Unknown Woman' for which she faked psychosis in order to be admitted to a psychiatric hospital was widely debated and by many was not regarded as art by the art world, but because it was debated by the art world it succeeded in breaking into the art world and is today regarded as art and Odell is regarded as an artist. Of course there are those who try and break out of this hegemony by refusing to play by the art world's unwritten rules. Andy Warhol with his factory was one, even though he is today totally embraced by the art world. Another example is Damien Hirst who, much like Warhol, pays people to create the physical manifestation of his ideas. He doesn't use galleries and other art world approved arenas to advertise his objects and instead sells them to private individuals. This liberal approach to capitalism is one way of attacking the hegemony of the art world. What does all this teach us about art? Probably that art is a fleeting and chimeric concept. We will always have art but for the most part we will only learn in retrospect what the art of our era will be, or was.

Chapter 2

The Making Of Meaning

Art is where we make meaning beyond language. Art consists in the making of meaning, through intelligent agency eliciting an aesthetic response. It's a means of communication where language is not sufficient to explain or describe its content. Art can render visible and known, what was previously unspoken. Because what art expresses and evokes and is in part ineffable, we find it difficult to define and delineate it. It's known throughout the experience of the audience as well as the intention and expression of the artist. The meaning is made by all participants and so we can never make it fully known or be known. It is multifarious and ongoing. Even a disagreement is a tension which is itself an experience of something.

Art drives the development of a civilisation both supporting the establishments and also preventing subversive messages from being silenced. Art leads, mirrors and reveals change in politics and morality. Art plays a central part in the creation of culture and is an outpouring of thought and ideas from it and so it cannot be understood in isolation from its context. Paradoxically however art can communicate beyond language and time, appealing to our common humanity and linking disparate communication. Perhaps if wider audiences engaged with a greater variety of the world's artistic traditions, it could engender increased tolerance and mutual respect. Another inescapable facet of art is that it is a commodity.

This fact feeds the creative process whether motivating the artist to form an item of monetary value or to avoid creating one or to artistically commodify the aesthetic experience. The commodification of art also affects who is considered qualified to create art, comment upon it and even define it, as those who benefit most strive to keep the value of art objects high. These influences must feed into the culture's understanding of what art is at any time, making thoughts about art culturally dependent. However, the commodification and the consequent closely guarded role of the artistic also gives rise to a counter culture often expressed through the creation of art that cannot be sold. The stratification of art by value and the resultant tension also adds to its meaning and the meaning of art to society.

Chapter 3

Communication And Beauty

Art is communication. Art is something we do, a verb. Art is an expression of our thoughts, emotions, intuitions and desires, but it is even more personal than that. It is about sharing the way to experience the world, which for many is an extension of personality. It is the communication of intimate concepts that cannot be faithfully portrayed by words alone, and because words are not enough we must find some other vehicle to carry our intent. However, this content that we instil on and in our chosen media is not in itself the art. Art is to be found in how the media has used the way in which the content is expressed. Also the question of beauty comes into question. What then is beauty? It is more than cosmetic. It is not about prettiness.

There are plenty of pretty pictures available at home furnishing stores, but these we might not refer to as beautiful, and it is not difficult to find works of artistic expression that we might agree are beautiful but not necessarily pretty. Beauty is rather a measure of effect, a measure of emotion. In the concept and context of art, beauty is the gauge of successful communication between participants, the conveyance of a concept between the artist and the perceiver. Beautiful art is about successfully portraying intended emotions, the desired concept, whether they be pretty and bright or dark and sinister, but neither the artist nor the observer can be certain of successful communication in the end. So beauty in art is eternally subjective.

Chapter 4

Beauty Versus Evil

Can we judge a work of art to be morally evil? It is not an accident that the artistic manifestations of Fascism were banal in the extreme. It is not an accident the argument goes, because works of art take their character from their makers. Art draws on what is instinctive about how artists view the world and the attitude that they take towards it. So Fascist art for example is bound to be bad because it instantiates Fascist values and a Fascist worldview. This amounts to claiming to produce laudable art or for a work to be artistically good if it is also morally bad. A piece of art Nazi propaganda which Hitler commissioned and helped to produce is not banal. This was the Swastika.

It was the art work that created most outrage. Depictions of the Swastika go back at least 10,000 years. To the Greeks, Japanese, Navajo Indians and many other cultures, the Swastika represented fire, fertility, the sun and circling stars. The word Swastika comes from a Sanskrit phrase meaning 'be well' and in German it was called 'the hooked cross'. This fits in well with the agenda of altering Christianity and replacing it with proper Aryan paganism. When the Nazi party were looking for symbols in art, the Swastika was close to hand.

In the Thule Society, a study group for German antiquity, the runes stood for occult energy and they adopted the Swastika as an emblem in 1918, and when its erstwhile practical wing, the Nazi party and Hitler, took credit for the final design of the Nazi flag which debuted in May 1920, basing it on a local party emblem designed by Fredrich Krohn, the effect, as Hitler declared later, was 'as if we had dropped a bomb'. It is commonly judged to be both beautiful and evil. The artistic and moral criteria tug in opposite directions. The basic evaluative question is whether the content nullifies its artistic mind as a work of propaganda. It was designed to spread the Nazi creed and mobilise the German people and present socialism as a political religion. Its image, doctrine and narrative, all aimed at entrenching its tenets: Germany as one nation, Hitler an inspired leader and the Third Reich to last a 1,000 years. Its most unsettling feature was how it presented a beautiful vision of Hitler and the New Germany that was morally evil.

It is a work of creative imagination, stylistically and formally innovative, its every detail contributes to its central vision and overall effect. It's also very beautiful. Its every detail designed to advance a vision that as history was to prove, falsified the true character of Hitler and National Socialism. It renders something that is evil, namely National Socialism beautiful and in so doing tempts the viewer to find attractive what is morally repugnant. There is a standard solution for tackling the problem of evaluation that arises when beauty is entwined with evil in a single work of art. The solution is known as Formalism. It puts an iron curtain between the form of an art work and its content. Form is shorthand for a work's formal features which in visual art includes balance, symmetry and perspective, all of which are usually achieved by the arrangement of shapes, lines and colours.

We take the formal features through our eyes in all visual arts, whereas an art work's formal features engage our senses, its content appeals to our mind and our emotions. It makes us think and feel, so content refers to the meaning of messages contained in works of art which their makers strive to express. Formalism asks that we evaluate art narrowly, solely in terms of its formal features, and to keep that assessment apart from any parallel evaluation of its emotional, political or other content, but is this actually possible? Suppose that we could make a purely aesthetic evaluation of a work's formal properties without discussing its content. That would let us ignore the Nazi propaganda in that work of art and judge it purely in terms of its formal qualities.

In that case we would know that it is morally bad. However, this is not a practical solution, let alone a morally acceptable one. In the best works of art, form is fused with the content. Consequently the value of such art work is not something that can be judged apart from the moral qualities of its content. Works of art enact their moral valuations. Form and content are not two discrete elements, so that the form of a well made work of art is integrated with its content. The two become indivisible.

There is a connection between the artistic value of works of art and the moral attitudes of those who bring them about which includes those who inspire and commission art as well as those who actually make it. This connection is necessary and contingent. This necessity isn't of the logical kind but an intrinsic sort of necessity, one that it is inherent in the work. The Nazi propaganda work of art is clearly of artistic value. It's extremely powerful, perhaps even a work of genius, but despite its mastery we must condemn it because it serves, is ruled by its vile vision, because it lies about the real nature of Nazi Germany. It presents as beautiful and good things that are categorically evil, namely Hitler and the National Socialism. It is impossible to ignore this fact when evaluating this art because the vision is essential to it being the work of art it is. We have seen that the pure approach to a work of art which raises, although it's a formalist approach, moral issues, is to sever aesthetic evaluation from moral evaluation and to assess the work in aesthetic terms alone.

This is impossible in judging it because the evil quality of its content is enacted by its form. The content is inextricable from its form and therefore it's impossible to judge the formal elements from the vision they instantiate. The beautiful vision of Hitler and Nazi Germany is the soul or essence of the work, the property that makes it the work of art it is. Hence in viewing it, it is impossible to disregard or to disengage or distance oneself from the vision. Therefore the work is bad as art.

Chapter 5

Grasping The World

Art is a way of grasping the world, not merely the physical world, which is what science attempts to do, but the whole world and specifically the human world, the world of society and spiritual experience. Art emerged long before cities and civilisation, yet in forms to which we can still directly relate, wall paintings in caves for example. Following the invention of photography, art cannot be simply defined on the basis of concrete tests like fidelity of representation or vague abstract concepts like beauty.

So how can art be defined in terms to both cave dwellers and modern city sophisticates? To do this we need to ask 'What does art do?' The answer is surely that it provokes an emotional response. Or it provokes that rather than a simple cognitive response. One way of approaching the problem of defining art could be to say that art consists of shareable ideas that have a shareable emotional input. Art need not produce beautiful objects or events, since a great piece of art could validly arouse emotions other than those aroused by beauty, such as terror, anxiety or laughter. Yet to devise an acceptable philosophical theory of art from this understanding means tackling the concept of emotion head on and philosophers have been notoriously reluctant to do this as it isn't easy.

Art is vitally important in maintaining broad standards in civilisation. Its pedigree deserves much more attention from philosophers. The fundamental difference between art and beauty is that art is about who has produced it whereas beauty depends on who is looking. Of course there are standards of beauty, that which is seen as traditionally beautiful. The game changers, the square pegs so to speak, are those who saw traditional standards of beauty and decided specifically to go against them, perhaps just to prove a point. Take the works of Picasso, Munch and the like, they have made a stand against these norms in their art. Its only function is to be experienced, appraised and understood, or not. The stand against the norms meant otherwise their art would have been like all other art.

Art is a means to state an opinion or a feeling or else to create a different view of the world whether it be inspired by the work of other people or something invented that is entirely new. Beauty is whatever aspect of that or anything else that makes an individual feel positive or grateful. Beauty alone is not art but art can be made of, about, or for beautiful things. Beauty can be found in a snowy mountain scene. Art is the photograph of it shown to family, the oil painting interpretation of it hung in a gallery. However, art is not necessarily positive. It can be deliberately hurtful or displeasing. It can make us think about or consider things we would rather not think about, but if it evokes an emotion in us then it is art.

Chapter 6

Mind And Art

Relationship between art and mind.

"Imagination abandoned by reason produces impossible monsters."

Art viewed as a product of the interaction between reason and imagination, both functions of the human mind, and these faculties provide the starting point for the exploration of the relationship between mind and art. This relationship of the human mind to art comprises complex categories of engagement with the visual. These cover themes such as the world we think we see and how we see this through art. We can think about the relationship of the human psyche to art too, and this can manifest itself in terms of both subject matter and approaches to interpreting art.

We may also consider the aesthetic and ways in which our sensual responses to an art work take precedence over our reasoned knowledge of it. This is by no means an exhaustive list of the possibilities of the theme of the mind in relation of art and to art, but an exploration of these aspects of art and mind helps to tease out how we use our brains to engage with and understand art. As a philosopher I am interested in the ambiguities in language and this also includes images as, like words, these can be understood in different ways. Whilst exploring the relationship between the external world and the art image, an internal cognitive change takes place. It is the processes that go on in the mind when we look at images including art works that are of interest.

What is important is that sometimes we can see something in a straightforward way, but at other times we notice a particular aspect, so we see it as something else. Art as an abstraction derives this abstraction from nature, whilst dreaming before it and thinking more of the creation which will result than of nature. Let's dig deeper to see how art relates to our inner selves or in other ways and words, the way in which the human psyche, whether that of the viewer or the artist, is manifest in art. Language is important as the words used to describe the art are key and these may be cultural differences and are also an important factor.

People from different continents show marked differences in their responses, whilst other interpretations remain constant across cultures. The point is about the way we look and interpret images, how this can be culturally determined and the importance of language in interpreting, separating art from artist. Having looked at the relationship between the physicality of the art and the physicality of the artist and how these interact through the theme of the art, we can attempt to dissemble the art work from the artist or at least show how they can operate on different levels. Firstly think about art as purely being about the aesthetic. Distinctions between the rational and the irrational and between reason and sentimental aesthetics being a mode of thought based on sensory perception seen as equal to rational or logical thoughts. Logic is based on verbal reasoning whereas aesthetics are based on the senses, in this case sight, regarding writing and speaking about visual experiences.

The language we use to describe art can be at odds with our experience of the art we see. This is the cornerstone of philosophy, which offers analysis of our ability to make individual judgements about aesthetics and how these underpin the concept of genius. This is seen as a way of assessing the quality of art works in terms of their beauty and purpose. There can be a range of aesthetic taste which also encourages the view that beautiful art arouses our sensations in the same way as moral judgements. Therefore aesthetics and ethics become intertwined and the concept of genius and taste are intrinsically linked with the moral character of the artist or viewer. Pinning down aesthetic judgement can be difficult. Indeed the history of art provides us with many instances where art works have provoked outrage.

Changes of opinion are due in fact to the reflective process of reasoning and that has resulted in the expansion of the category beautiful. Different methods of representation in figurative art have also tested the relationship between art outrage and aesthetic judgement. In the primary of the aesthetic promoted the view of art for art's sake, seeing parallels between painting and music, pictures which underscore by their titles the primary of the tonal harmony, whether aural or visual. Art should be independent of all claptrap, should stand alone and appeal to the artistic sense of eye without confronting or confounding it with emotions entirely foreign to it as devotion, piety, joy, patriotism and the like. These have no kind of concern with it and are called works, arrangements and harmonies. Also high prices for art can be defended for the knowledge gained by the work of a lifetime, and art with a high price tag is accepted and often admired as tonal arrangements and experimentations in the representations of form.

Chapter 7

Art Asks A Question

Some years ago I went looking for art. To begin my journey I went to an art gallery. At that stage art to me was whatever I found in an art gallery. I found paintings mostly and because they were in a gallery I recognised them as art. A particular painting was of one colour and large. I observed a further piece that did not have an obvious label. It was also of one colour but gigantically large occupying one complete wall of the very high and spacious room and standing on small roller wheels.

On closer inspection I saw that it was a movable wall, not a piece of art. Why could one piece of work be considered art and the other not? The answer could perhaps be in the criteria to decide if some artifact is indeed art, that art pieces function only as pieces of art as their creators intended, but were they beautiful? Beauty is frequently associated with art. There is sometimes an expectation of encountering a beautiful art work when going to see a work of art, be it a painting, sculpture, book or performance. Of course the expectation quickly changes as one widens the range of installations encountered. Can we define beauty? Let me try to suggest that beauty is the capacity of an artifact to evoke a pleasurable emotional response.

This might be categorised as the like response. Looking at any art is skill of course in the construction but what is the skill in presenting a work as art? So I began to reach a definition of art. A work of art is that which asks a question which a non art object such as a wall does not. What am I? What am I communicating? The response both of the creator artist and of the recipient audience varies but it invariably invokes a judgement, a response to the invitation to answer. The answer goes towards deciphering a deeper question. Who am I? Which goes towards defining humanity.

Chapter 8

The Elusiveness of Art

Art periods such as Classical, Byzantine, Neo-Classical, Romantic, Modern and Post-Modern, reflect the changing nature of art in social and cultural contexts and shifting values are evident in varying content, forms and styles. These changes are encompassed more or less in sequence by imitationalist theories of art claiming a distinctiveness for art that inextricably links its instances with acts of observation, without which all that could exist would be material counterparts or mere real things rather than art works. Notwithstanding the competing theories, works of art can be seen to possess family resemblance linking very difference instances of art.

Identifying instances of art is relatively straightforward but a definition of art that includes all possible cases is elusive. Consequently art has been claimed to be an open concept. Capitalised art appears in general use in the 19th century with Fine Art, whereas art has a history of precious applications such as music, poetry, tragedy, dance and literature, media arts and even gardening, which can provide epiphanies of co-dependence. Art is then perhaps anything presented for our own aesthetic contemplation. Gaining our aesthetic interest is at least a necessary requirement of art. Sufficiency for something to be art requires significance to art appreciation and art appreciators which endures as long as tokens or types of the art work persist.

Paradoxically such significance is something attributed to objects neither intended as art nor especially intended to be perceived aesthetically, for instance votive, devotional, commemorative or utilitarian artifacts. Furthermore aesthetic interests can be eclipsed by dubious investment practices and social kudos. When combined with celebrity and harmful forms of narcissism they can egregiously affect artistic authenticity. These interests can be overriding and spawn products masquerading as art. Then it is up to discerning observers to spot any fads, fakes or fantasies.

Chapter 9

Acceptance

For some, art is nothing more and nothing less than the creativity of individuals to express their understanding of some aspects of private or public life, like love, conflict, fear or pain. Reading literature, poetry, enjoying a concert, or contemplating a drawing, we are often emotionally inspired by the moment and intellectually stimulated by the thought process that follows. At a moment of discovery we humbly realise our views may be shared by thousands, even millions, across the globe. This is due in large part to the mass media's ability to control and exploit our emotions. The commercial success of a performance or production becomes the metric by which art is almost exclusively gauged. Quality in art has been sadly reduced to equating great art with sale of books, number of views, or the downloading of recordings.

Too bad if personal sensibilities about a particular piece of art are lost in the greater rush for immediate acceptance. So where does that leave the subjective notion that beauty can still be found in art? If beauty is the outcome of a process by which art gives pleasure to our senses then it should remain a matter of discernment, even if outside forces clamour to take control of it. In other words nobody including the art critic should be able to tell the individual what is beautiful and what is not. The world of art is one of the constant tensions between preserving individual tastes and promoting popular acceptance.

Chapter 10

Art As Experience

Works of art may elicit a sense of wonder or cynicism, hope or despair, adoration or spite. It may be direct or complex, subtle or explicit, intelligible or obscure, and the subject matter and approaches to the creation of art are bounded only by the imagination of the artist. Consequently it can be believed that defining art based upon its content is a doomed enterprise. Now a theme in aesthetics, the study of art, is the claim that there is a detachment or distance between works of art and the flow of everyday life. Thus works of art rise like islands from a current of more pragmatic concerns. When you step out of a river and onto an island you have reached your destination, Similarly the aesthetic attitude requires us to treat artistic experience as an end in itself. Art asks us to arrive with an empathy of preconceptions and attend to the way in which we experience the work of art.

Although a person can have an aesthetic experience of a natural scene, flavour or texture, art is different in that it is produced. Therefore art is the intentional communication of an experience as an end in itself. The content of that experience in its cultural context may determine whether the art work is popular or ridiculed, significant or trivial, but it is art either way.

One of the initial reactions to this approach may be that it seems overly broad. Some definitions would exclude graphics used in advertising or political propaganda as they are created as a measure and means to an end and not for their own sakes. Furthermore communication is not the best word for it implies an unwarranted intention about the content represented. Aesthetic responses are often underdetermined by the artist's intentions.

Chapter 11

Majority Versus Minority

Human beings appear to have a compulsion to categorise, organise and define. We seek to impose order on a welter of sense impressions and memories, seeing regularities and patterns in repetitions and associations, always on the lookout for correlations, eager to determine cause and effect so that we might give sense to what might otherwise seem random and inconsequential. However, particularly in the last century we have also learned to take pleasure in the reflection of unstructured perceptions. Our artistic ways of seeing and listening have expanded to encompass disharmony and irregularity.

This has meant that culturally an ever widening gap has grown between the attitudes and opinions of the majority who continue to define art in traditional ways, having to do with order, harmony, representation, and the minority who look for originality, who try to see the world anew and strive for difference, and whose critical practice is rooted in abstraction. In between there are many who abjure both extremes and who find and give pleasure, both in defining a personal vision and in practising traditional art craftmanship. There will always be a challenge to traditional concepts of art from the shock of the new and tensions around the appropriateness of our understanding.

That is how things should be as innovators push the boundaries. At the same time we will continue to take pleasure in the beauty of a mathematical equation, a finely turned machine, a successful scientific experiment, an accomplished poem, a striking portrait and the sound world of a symphony. We apportion significance and meaning to what we find of value and wish to share with our fellow human beings. Our art and our definition of beauty reflect our human nature and the multiplicity of our creative efforts. In the end because of our individuality and our varied histories and traditions our debates will always be inconclusive. If we are wise we will look and listen with an open spirit and sometimes with a wry smile, always celebrating the diversity of human imaginings and achievements.

Chapter 12

Beauty In Art

What we perceive as beautiful does not offend us on any level. It is a personal judgement, a subjective opinion. A memory from once we gazed upon something beautiful, a sight ever so pleasing to the senses or to the eye oft time stays with us forever. I shall not forget walking into Balzac's house in France. The scent of lilies was so overwhelming I had a numinous moment. The intensity of the emotion evoked may not be possible to explain. I do not think a flaxen painting, a sunset or how the light streaming through a stained glass window are beautiful. The power of the sights created an emotional reaction in me. I do not expect or concern myself that others will agree with me or not.

Can all agree that an act of kindness is beautiful? A thing of beauty is a whole, elements coming together making it so. A single brush stroke of a painting does not alone create the impact of beauty but all together it becomes beautiful. A perfect flower is beautiful, when all of its petals together form its perfection. A pleasant, intoxicating scent is also a part of the beauty. I have simply come away with the idea that I am the beholder whose eye it is in when thinking about the question, 'what is beauty'. Suffice to say my private assessment of what strikes me as beautiful is all I need to know. It has been said that beauty is the promise of happiness but this doesn't get to the heart of the matter.

Whose beauty are we talking about and whose happiness? From a different perspective of view we can see that beauty is truly in the eye of the beholder. It may cross our lips to speak of the nature of beauty in billowy language but we do so entirely with a forked tongue if we do so seriously. The aesthetics of representing beauty ought not to fool us into thinking that beauty as some abstract concept truly exists. It requires a viewer and a context and the value we place on certain combinations of colours or sounds over others speaks of nothing more than performance.

Our desire for pictures moving or otherwise is because our organs developed in such away. A snake for example would have no use for the visual world. I am thankful to have human art over snake art, alien to us, but I would be no doubt amazed at serpentine art. It would require an intellectual sloughing of many conceptions we take for granted. For that, considering the possibility of this extreme thought is worthwhile. If snakes could write poetry or literature, what would it be?

Chapter 13

Definition

The two questions, what is art and what is beauty, are different types and shouldn't be conflated. With boring predictability almost all contemporary discussions of art lapse into a relative of, whereby they go to annoying lengths to demonstrate how open minded they are and how incredibly loose the concept of art is. If art is whatever you want it to be, can we not just end the conversation there? It's a done deal. I will throw playdough onto a canvas and we can pretend to display our modern credentials of acceptance and insight. This just doesn't work and we all know it. If art has to mean anything there has to be some working definition of what it is.

If art can be anything to anybody at any time, then there ends the discussion. What makes art special and worth discussing is that it stands above or outside everyday things such as food, paintwork or sounds. Art comprises special exceptional dishes, paintings and music. So what then is a definition of art? Briefly I believe there must be at least two considerations to label something as art. The first is there must be something recognisable in the way of author to audience reception. This is to say there must be the recognition that something was made for an audience of some kind to receive, discuss or enjoy. Implicit in this point is the evident recognisability of what the art actually is. In other words the author doesn't have to tell you it's art when you otherwise wouldn't have any idea.

The second point is simply the recognition of skill. Some obvious skill has to be involved in making all art. These in my view would be the minimum requirements to a definition of art. Even if you disagree with the particulars, some definition is required to make anything at all art. Otherwise what are we even discussing? I am breaking the mould and ask for brass tacks.

Chapter 14

Art And The Audience

What exactly does the loss of perspective on art mean? It means that with time art has become more available yet more difficult to comprehend and admire. This in turn means that even so, as there is more art for people to see, that doesn't necessarily translate into people actually enjoying it. Does this imply that there may be something wrong with conceptual or abstract art? Absolutely not. The answer to the difficulty is not to make all art works completely transparent, saying with this that art must lack its own intrinsic intellectual or aesthetic values. The answer is thought to lie in understanding a view especially concerning the relationship between the artist, the work of art and the spectator.

We need to take a step back and try to understand what the claimed essence of this relationship is, whether it matters and if it may or may not have implications for the construction of personal artistic values, as well as for the values of society as a whole. Any work of art poses a challenge to spectators. The challenge is to fully understand and appreciate that the whole value of what is presented to them cannot be reduced to a single cause alone, be it pleasure, politics, mathematics or whatever.

Why would anyone think this to be a challenge? If it is such a daunting task, why would we care for art? Shouldn't a painting for example be first a pleasure for the eye rather than a challenge for the intellect? Yet even if many or most of the paintings out there can give enormous amounts of sheer pleasure when beheld, it is not true that grasping a painting only requires one to cultivate the eye. The process of apprehending a painting assumes the existence of certain values such as ideals of beauty or the sublime, as in the case of an artist's portrayal of goodness and so on, that must be present in the mind and soul of anyone who wants to appreciate the painting to the fullest extent. It does not matter that the intention of the artist may be other than that of simply exciting or feeding the eye, for say, beauty, can certainly be found on grounds other than that of colour or the harmony of the form.

We can rightfully begin to have at least the suspicion that such values are the subject matter or maybe even the essence we apprehend in the work of art. We may accept then that these values coexist with the physical reality of the painting. We can then perceive the painting as something that can be esteemed. No matter if what type of art it is, it not only presupposes the existence of values for both artist and audience. It also proposes to the observer a particular view upon such values and sometimes suggests the recognition of new ones. In other words art works not only presuppose values but in doing so asks the spectator to become critical of his own values, assumptions, and prejudices.

These values are composed into the art work not only for the viewers to appreciate or value them but also to mould values into them and from them begin to remould even the foundation of society when intellectual bases do not have to be changeless. So at the same time as it moulds culture,art can mould the way society perceives itself and also shape the ways it would like to be perceived in the future. Nevertheless the comparatively solid ground upon which culture is built is valued in the everyday sense of the term.

Chapter 15

Growth Of Art

In the early 90s Russian painting's purpose was to portray art as the greatest expression of the human spirit. They were not the first and certainly not the last to propose this link between art and spirituality. Before then Romantic thought in general had developed an approach to aesthetics that highlighted the incompatible nature of human life and modern industrial creations. Nevertheless the 20th century has witnessed such a variety of art concepts and artistic production that assuming a vision like that of the Russian painters may seem arbitrary and even naïve, just because their vision can argue neither in favour of, nor against the value of 20th century radical aesthetic trends such as conceptual art and the like.

The artistic freedom in at least most of the Western world for the past hundred years has had no precedent in history. Yet at the same time as all sorts of artistic manifestations and movements have appeared, any pretence of finding objective values in art or even implying their existence has become more and more unlikely. There are two main reasons for this.

First is the acknowledgement of the artist's work as a form of expression which above all is subjective in the sense that it does not obey received rules on form or taste. An absolute respect for this subjectivity is required in order for the art appreciator to obtain the most from each individual artistic expression. This respect has made the work of art untouchable in many ways and more often than not has isolated the viewer from the purpose of the artist. Secondly the growth of all forms of artistic movements and ways of expression has resulted in the massive proliferation of the art works available to the person on the street, making it a herculean task to keep up even with the mainstream of art.

Even as art works of all kinds have become more accessible to all, there seems to be a loss of perspective with respect to aesthetic thought and purpose since the birth of Impressionism in the second half of the 19th century. Nevertheless it is believed that Romanticism's claim that human creativity is a life force has actually been undermined by the substantial growth of artistic movements throughout the past century and in this one too. This growth needs to be accompanied by a better understanding of art and art work and not only be focusing on the quantitative growth of the industry.

Chapter 16

Art Movements

Art movements is the name given to certain styles of art that are made at particular times by artists who share such things as artistic ideals, styles and methods of approaches. Some art movements are named in retrospect long after the movement happens, such as the Renaissance or the Baroque, while some are named by the artists themselves as they form a group, such as Futurism or Surrealism, and some are named accidentally or derogatively by critics, such as Impressionism and Cubism. Some art movements include artists who all agree and discuss their principles such as Dada or Stijip, while others have little in common but are simply labelled by later generations, for instance Post-Impressionism.

These movements mainly relate to Western art development. A common aspect of all art movements is that they occur during a specific period of time over months, years or many years. So for instance an artist today might paint in the Rococo style but would not be part of the Rococo movement per se, as that period has passed. Since the 20th century there have been more art movements and faster changes between them than at any other period in history. Many of the more recent art movements are not even clearly defined. This will occur when more time has elapsed. Most movements begin when certain avante-garde artists break with accepted rules or traditions and create something markedly different from art that has been previously produced.

Some art movements are deliberately formed as a reaction against a recent movement, such as Pop Art in the 1960s in response to Abstract Expressionism. Some movements seek to emulate previous periods of art, like the early Baroque emulated the High Renaissance, or many artists took mediaeval examples. The list of movements begin with the Prehistoric, followed by Ancient Greek and Roman, Byzantine, Mediaeval, Early Renaissance, Northern Renaissance, High Renaissance, Mannerism, Dutch, Golden Age, Baroque, Rococo, Neo-Classicism, Romanticism, Realism, Impressionism, Post-Impressionism, German Expressionism, Favism, Cubism, Art Nouveau, Art Deco, New Impressionism, Futurism, Surrealism, Abstract Impressionism, Colour Field, Pop Art, Performance Art, Minimalism and Conceptualism.

The position of the artist is humble. He is essentially a channel and creativity takes courage and if the artist could say it in words there would be no reason to paint and there is sensitivity in technique. Covering the artistic span of 18,000 years are some of the most innovative and ground-breaking works of art ever made including portraits, sculpture, nudes, landscapes, allegories, myths and religious stories, and each expresses powerful messages or styles showing individual artists' approaches and intentions. Every art work demonstrates uniqueness and particular skills or cutting-edge qualities and the artists who created them were sometimes derided or vilified when they first produced or presented their work. Yet by doing something different and refusing to conform these artists changed the path of the history of art. While in retrospect many of these works to contemporary eyes may seem tame or not particularly revolutionary when they were originally created, many were seen as shocking or irrelevant.

Depicted in numerous ways by different artists, many of the same or similar themes have featured throughout history in a diverse range of contexts. Exploring art throughout themes can enhance our understanding of the intentions and ideas it represents. Themes in art are often messages about life, society or human nature, and are usually implied rather than explicitly stated. Not identical with the particular subject, themes are often ambiguous or vague. Certain themes such as landscape or religion or colour are more prevalent during particular movements or time periods. From drawing with charcoal or screen printing and from frescoes to foreshortening, since art was first produced artists have evolved countless techniques and methods and explored the evolution of the artistic methods used throughout history, such as painting with oils, underpainting, etching, the lost wax method and impasto. Many artists have invented certain techniques along with changes in approach as key developments.

Chapter 17

Forms Of Art

The term art can be used in a different number of ways, each with a different meaning or sense. Some may use the term honourifically as when viewing a painting they exclaim 'Now that's what I call art'. The term may also be used ironically or metaphorically. Most uses of the term however are in a classificatory sense implying that all art works or art forms are to be classified under one heading. In discussions about art it is easy when presenting an argument to unknowingly jump from the classificatory sense to the honourific sense of the term. In its classificatory sense the art is shorthand for the term art form. An art form is a category term that gathers works together based on the medium used and the manner of application. Thus theatre is an art form, as is painting, sculpture, dance, literature etc.

Art also contains subheadings which distinguish particular works according to their genre, style or school of presentation. As designators of categories, art forms are unique and have no counterpart in any other categorical system. Thousands of years ago it was recognised that all works of art have a medium of presentation, a manner of presentation. These also have an object of presentation and these three aspects of a work allow us to determine its art form, the category of art in which it is placed. It is also one reason why we seldom confuse everyday items with works of art.

We distinguish one art form from another by attending to each of these three aspects for the works in question. For example an oil painting and a water colour are different forms, and while each may present the same subject they involve different media which require different methods of application and so involve different manners of presentation too. The medium of a work is most often the mean of identifying its form.

Chapter 18

Values Of Art

What is said about the existence of values within a work of art? Although it may seem clear that values are present in the artist as well as in the spectator it is not necessarily clear that a work of art must represent such values in itself. Thus it is fair to ask if it is possible that such a work of art can be free of any form of values whatsoever? Is it possible then having been said about the values being at the core of art, it wouldn't be true? If so we must ask ourselves what then is the foundation of a work of art? With this question we only want to say that an aspect of aesthetics is the expression of value, albeit maybe the most fundamental aspect. Therefore we must proceed to ask whether it is possible to have works of art that are devoid of value.

To answer this let's begin by asking what exactly happens during the creation process and if during that process the artist or creator always undertakes a conscious labour. The first thing that may come to mind is that many artists use techniques in their work that apply chance as a basic principle so that the artist might distance himself from societal values or at least any conscious attempt to manifest them in the art work. We could say for example that a process like that of action painting such as dripping paint onto canvas can have in no way completely predictable results even if the artist tries his or her best to control them, which they often do not. However although the technique itself may be random or unintentional and elements may be random, it is still true that the artist never loses intimacy, or better a bond, with the painting.

This word bond obviously expresses the closeness that exists between creator and creation and it would be absurd to think that any such bond can lack all conscious intention. The art work cannot be completely detached from the artist. The artist can never be an outsider to his own work for the painting or any other art work as an artistic creation will in a sense be always nothing more than an extension of the creator.

We can see then that it does not matter what kind of art work we might be talking about, be it completely realistic or made by dripping paint, a happening or performance, the artist can never free himself from the artist's responsibility as a creator. This makes it important, and impossible for him to become an outsider or a bystander to his work; one cannot be a foreigner in one's own land. In more precise terms the artist cannot achieve with his art what many would call objectivity, any supposed absolute distance between the artist and his work will always rather be by degree only. The artist may only vary the technique or the intention behind the art work in order to produce different responses in the spectator, but it is just impossible for artists to be alien to their work. This is a very distinct conclusion for it means that the creative process is non objective. This means that it is impossible for anyone to describe the artistic creative process through a series of events that have to take place in order for the artistic creation to appear and hence not generalisable in nature.

In common language there is just no recipe for making art and not only does such a recipe not exist, it cannot exist. There is one reason and that is it and why an artist creates while an entrepreneur produces and why we don't have factories for paintings as we have for prints. Furthermore it is subjectivity within the work of art that determines the whole significance of the creating. By reflecting upon the necessarily subjective character of the process we can recognise that what takes place during the process is an encounter with the artist with an inner necessity to express himself. This necessarily cannot itself be explained by any tangible need but by the artist's own spiritual reality. This reality is esteemed in or valued within itself and also for the values it presents when expressed to others.

When we acknowledge this a concept becomes quite enlightening. Moving to the perspective of the viewer, since we have just confirmed the presence of values within the painting it becomes quite reasonable to say that since we the viewers esteem values, we subsequently esteem and appreciate the painting for its value charged content as we can call it. Having discussed the importance of spirituality and values and their relationship with art it has become clear that in order for a bystander to be able to appreciate art in any form he must be open not only to the expressions of the artist's unique spirituality, his values and personal aesthetics, he must also be prepared to embrace that reality to some degree.

This also obviously implies that what is meant to be conveyed by the artist through his work must actually be understood by the observer. This encounter proposes a communication of sorts, or a mediator, between artist and observer and this can only take place if the observer is aware of his own spiritual reality and the values it contains. This awareness is most definitely the main condition that must exist not only for the spectator to appreciate the painting that hangs in front of him but in general for a society as a whole to embrace and as a means to understand and discuss its own values, that is as a means to conduct a critical appraisal of the place of art in society. Most important of all, values do not exist in some obvious reality that escapes all reach or consequences for practical or daily life. Although it may come across in this way, this is just a result of the same problem. Society as a whole has become so short-sighted that spiritual reality is imagined by many in the same way they imagine facing fairy tales, as bearing no direct relation to everyday life.

As a conclusion we must acknowledge that values are present intrinsically in works of art, just by virtue of their being art works. This however is not to be taken lightly for it means that the true apprehension of the artist as a creator demands a state of openness on behalf of the viewer. This state of openness is not something that necessarily exists and may not exist at all if he who observes is not aware of what he is observing. Of course an acknowledgement of values as intrinsic to art also sets boundaries for the artist himself, who can only call himself an artist if he accepts his own spirituality or values it as the force from which he forges a material expression. Altogether even as artistic value continues to reach beyond aesthetic pleasure it increasingly becomes evident that it is a force that enhances and perpetuates the human spirit. Art that deserves to be called art will always give to both maker and observer a sense of fulfilment or completeness. This is what makes it by far the most outstanding expression of the human spirit.

Chapter 19

Three Fallacies

There is a better way, but before this way is demonstrated we must unpack three great fallacies of aesthetics. There are widespread interdependent claims about art and to demonstrate the fallacy of art, one will show the weakness of the other two. The first fallacy is that art works possess the quality called creativity but creativity as opposed to creating is not making activity. It is a thinking thing, a thinking activity. This is one reason that artists experiment with conceptual art. Yet although it may be hard for some to swallow, creativity no more exists in a painting say, than colour exists in a painting.

Colour exists in the perceiver's response to light of various wavelengths and the pigments in paintings merely reflect particular wavelengths which the eye allows the mind to see as the colours. So too, the creative act takes place in the mind of the viewer and is often accompanied by the shock of recognition. That is why there is no objection that appreciating art is fundamentally the cognitive act of grasping connections. Therefore when someone describes a work as creative they are saying something about themselves and perhaps about the artist. This may also be true when a work is described as lacking creativity, but could anyone recognise creativity if they did not have the capacity to think creatively?

Philosophically creativity is not a defining condition for categorising a work as art, although it may play a role in the criticism of particular works, that is it may be used to describe some works as good and some works as bad. If the first argument has been persuasive then the second fallacy will seem to be superfluous. The second fallacy is that works we call art must be artefacts and they must be man-made. Found objects and paintings by animals are excluded. Yet if we accept that creativity exists in the minds of the viewers we can understand that art need not be man-made.

The postulate that they must be is coveted by some aestheticians to honour the supremacy of human activity as human cognitivity appreciating art works that are not man made. For aestheticians the point of art is to satisfy some aesthetic function, then by definition it is not a work of art. The point of art is that it is art, although this might sound circular.

Chapter 20

Modernism

A spectre is haunting philosophy, the spectre of modernism. Constantly philosophers eager to associate themselves with a defining era have tried to produce a new literary school, movement or cultural condition and often succeeded only in heading back towards modernism. For instance in recent years theorists have worked their way out of post-modernism the only way they know how, back towards modernism.

We are confronted with the apparent reality that we cannot theorise away from modernism. It was a tendency in art, architecture and literature which emphasised sincerity, rationality and a desire to break the shackles of tradition. In the late 20th century it was largely displace by post-modernism, a tendency characterised by irony, playfulness and a claim that there is not one single truth, but many competing perspectives of equal validity. Is post-modernism dead? If so how can this new cultural condition be described?

Have we entered a post-modern age? This is actually an enquiry into the mentality of contemporary society. Attempting to define the current cultural climate is difficult at best, but it also raises concerns about society's aspirations. Having journeyed through modernism and post-modernism we wish to travel to the theory beyond, before this elusive new culture has even had time to solidify. In fact today's ism if indeed there is one, appears to be an amalgamation of previous theories.

Chapter 21

The Afterlives Of Modernism

Following on from post-modernism was the less articulate post-post-modernism. That is various post-modernism theories have emerged, none of which have been as influential or enduring as the 20th century's philosophical offspring. Yet they continue to proliferate in various manifestations. Replacing post-modernism comes pseudo-modernism, this culture being dependent on the individual and on individual action.

Pseudo-modern cultural products do not and cannot exist unless the individual intervenes physically in them. Then developed the manifest of re-modernism as a criticism of post-modernism and a revival of sorts of modernism. It was considered anti-anti-art, that is it re-emphasised the importance of figurative painting and criticised post-modernism for its purported lack of appreciation of originality, claiming post-modernism to be lost in the cul-de-sac of idiocy.

The idea of post-modernism is its claim to be the apex of art history while simultaneously denying the values that make art works worth having in the first place. It purports to address significant issues but actually has no meaning beyond the convoluted dialogue it holds with itself. If there is any innovation and vision in post-modernism it is in the field of art. Marketing post-modernism is destined for the dustbin of history.

Meanwhile re-modernism characterises itself as the movement that re-applies modernist thinking to contemporary society. The post-modernist takes the original principles of modernism and re-applies them, highlighting vision as opposed to formalism. Re-modernism discards and replaces post-modernism because of its failures to answer or address any importance to issues of being a human being. Re-modernism embodies a spiritual depth and meaning and brings to an end an age of scientific materialism, nihilism and spiritual bankruptcy. It can be seen as the precursor to the new sincerity movement that would emerge in the present decade.

Disavowing both modernism and post-modernism and proclaiming that we must liberate ourselves form the inertia resulting from a century of modernist ideology and ideological naivety, which is the cynical insincerity of its antonymous bastard child. Yet like many other self-invented cultural movements, meta-modernism has not succeeded in dominating social thought.

Chapter 22

Today's Cultural Philosophy

In response to post-modernism, nihilistic tendencies and more sincere movements have since emerged that reflect the genuine artistic concerns of modernism. Yet just as those vestiges of modernism have appeared in recent years openly criticising post-modernism's lack of any perceived beliefs, sincerity, or appreciation of art history, various reactionaries have started to criticise the new wave of sincerity movements and the artists they produce. In contrast to the modernist artist who was an impassioned, expressive figure, Pop art idols saw the artist's persona as mechanistic and hollow, able to be easily appropriated into his art, cementing the theory that anybody could do it.

The trend against personal genius really took off in the latter half of the 20th century with artists attempting to portray the artistic self as hollow and chameleon like, bereft of any true unchanging substance. It was argued that in place of post-modernism, lack of belief structures and lack of grand meta-narratives, the new sincerity movement re-emphasises genuine issues and beliefs, saying that all across the pop culture spectrum the emphasis on sincerity and authenticity that has arisen has made it ironically cool to care about spirituality, family and the environment and the country. The irony that defined the era of post-modernism faded out considerably with the move to a new sincerity movement which, tired of expressive irony, seeks to move towards a more impassioned sensibility with much the same ideals as the modernists, but is unlikely to be wholly embraced by a culture that is used to post-modern irony.

Chapter 23

Yesterday's Cultural Philosophy

Many philosophers have for instance noted that the movement of romanticism did not completely die and has not yet come to its end. Some remnants of romanticism may still be found in the popular media, but in such a mangled, disfigured form that they achieve the opposite of romanticism's original purpose. The last remnants of romanticism are sneaking apologetically on the outskirts of our culture, so post-modernism replicates characteristics of romanticism.

The persistence of romantic thought and literary practice into the late 20th century is evident in many contexts, from the philosophical and ideological abstractions of literary theory to the thematic and formal preoccupations of contemporary fiction and poetry. History boasts a succession of defining epochs, each with its own idiosyncratic collection of subcultural movements and enduring metaphors. It is no surprise that enthusiasts for post-modernism should wish to define its own period and identify and isolate its artists in order that it may take its place in the stately procession of history. This self-definition seems to stem from a psychological and cultural desire for both individual and collective creative significance.

An essential flaw of post-modernism is exactly that it attempts to locate itself as a historical period. From the very outset post-modernism was self-conscious about its identity as a period, conscious of its own historicity because it conceived of itself as historical. The problem invariably became that the post-modernists attempted to prematurely characterise themselves, interfering with the natural unfolding of a historical social perspective. The argument is that the ultimate failure of post-modernism is its eagerness to historicise itself before it has really finished, perhaps due to a sense of historical envy.

The act of hastily pre-historicising one's present is the notion that contemporary ideas and ideologies are unlikely to be given enough time to solidify and cannot serve as frames of reference for human actions. Post-modernism became fundamentally concerned with the perpetual present and by its very name labelled itself the thing that followed all else significant, effectively problematising its relationship with history but also cementing modernism as the place from which all theory extended. History could be divided as pre or post modernism. Post-modernism was also the theory that engaged with past artefacts that could produce nothing completely innovative but could only appropriate and use pre-existing cultural creations. As a result, post-modernism arose with the dreaded notion of the end of genius of consequential theories of art. Since the end of modernism is constantly aligned with the death of literature and the death of enquiry of great consequence, it is perhaps no surprise that society has been unable to wholly relinquish modernism's ghost.

Chapter 24

Tomorrow's Cultural Philosophy

In recent years instead of one theory or philosophy dominating, contemporary culture has indeed seen a notable blend of fragments of various ideas, styles and motivations, becoming a smorgasbord of theories and philosophies. Perhaps this chaos is why cultural theorists seem so eager to offer a particular label to the current cultural matrix. But where previous social and political changes instituted new dominant ideologies, the proliferation of voices and schemes has today fractured the stable ground upon which overriding ideas might be formed and cemented in place. Yet the ongoing trend of nostalgia, the act of perpetually looking backwards to modernism, has created an Orpheus type society.

In mythology Orpheus looked back at his love, rescuing her from Hades, and in so doing lost her, so the gaze of Orpheus is a metaphor for society's continued act of looking back towards the past, though the past is already lost in the act of looking back. Melancholy occurs once ordinary mourning fails and manifests itself as a pathological attachment to a lost object. The past however is the ultimate lost object. It is absolutely inaccessible and the attempt to replicate modernism ignores the fact that modernism emerged under specific historical, political and social conditions. However similar the new concepts may appear to be modernism, modernism as it was cannot be replicated. However close we come to injecting culture with significant doses of sincerity it does not act as a mirror to modernism. Yet it seems as though many people are anxious to return to tradition and to do so are creating their own theories of the resulting culture before the culture has even had time to take form. Genuine philosophy is developed or understood in hindsight, that is, a cultural movement can only be philosophically understood at its ending, in retrospect.

When philosophy paints its gloomy picture, then a form of life has grown old. It cannot be rejuvenated by the gloomy picture but only be understood. Perhaps we fear we have reached the end of history and so our own era will not be suitably defined. Perhaps we are too fixated on the afterlives of previous theories and too eager to clumsily and hopelessly create new theories. Yet out of all the theories clumsily floating around, can we truly tell which ones will solidify long enough to define the current and upcoming era? In a culture that has become defined by instantaneousness and fragmentation we have become too brash with ideologies. The idea that we are living in a liquid time where nothing solidifies long enough to become a dominant ideology. Culture cannot be adequately captured while it is still liquid before it has time to solidify. Rather a culture and its philosophies can be expected to form itself in its own time.

Chapter 25

The Art Prophet

Marcel Duchamp was known as the art prophet because before him a work of art was an artefact, a physical object, but after him it was an idea, a concept. He did to art what Einstein did to physics and Darwin to religion, each destroyed the foundations of a brilliant subject. Duchamp approached the demolition of the art establishment and the pretentiousness of artists with the cold-eyed calculation of a saboteur. The art of his maternal grandfather filled their house and from a young age he absorbed artistic sensibilities. He took up art and became a painter and his brief career as a pure painter subliminally culminated with his masterpiece 'Nude ascending a staircase' which he submitted to the Cubist Salon des Independents but the organisers of the exhibition asked him to withdraw the painting or paint over the title. He promptly went to the showroom and removed it from the exhibition.

This was a turning point in his life which he thereafter devoted to seeking an answer to two questions, 'What is to be deemed as acceptable as art, and who decides?' He had two strategic objectives, first to destroy the hegemony exerted by an establishment which claimed the right to decide what was and what was not to be deemed a work of art and second to puncture the pretentious claims of those who called themselves artists and in so doing assumed that they possessed extraordinary skills and unique gifts of discrimination and taste.

Tactically he sought to make a very bold and very public gesture by seeking to submit some totally outrageous entry under conditions the art establishments would be forced either to accept under their own rules or to break these rules, giving reasons for rejection. He saw the perfect opportunity in an exhibition whose rules explicitly stated that all works of art submitted would be exhibited. He discovered an ideal exhibit, a standard flat backed white porcelain urinal, and gave it the title 'Fountain'. It is the only submission to the exhibition which is now remembered since often having been on display for a short while, the organising committee suitably outraged, rejected it. However he had succeeded beyond his wildest expectations and achieved the notoriety he was after and it shifted the thinking of the art world.

Chapter 26

The Philosophical Aftermath of Duchamp

Over the centuries hundreds of artists have produced thousands of accepted masterpieces which adorn museums and galleries worldwide. Until the early 20th century it had seemed fairly clear what these works had in common. They were all physical artefacts such as paintings, sculptures, engravings and etchings which showed exemplary craftsmanship and were representations considered beautiful, interesting or inspiring. Today it seems that anything goes in art galleries: animal carcasses, unmade beds, comic book paintings, rows of bricks, live performances, created landscapes and more. Whatever, it would be totally unreasonable to claim that such a dramatic change could be laid at the feet of Marcel Duchamp. It would equally be unreasonable to ignore the impact made by him. It also seems ill advised to claim as philosophers did once that this change means that art is now dead. On the contrary art seems to be flourishing as never before.

What has happened is that there has been a progressive demolition of practically all the conditions which had been regarded as mandatory for something to be considered a work of art. Art no longer has to represent anything, nor even to be beautiful, although it of course can be, nor required exemplary skill for its production, although that may be so too. Neither does it have to be made by the putative artist, who can simply put forward an idea for somebody else to make or perform. Why one should then be regarded as an artist and the other not, is an interesting philosophical question in itself.

Another question is if it were possible to make exact physical copies of art using 3D printing why should only the original be a work of art? It cannot be the case that absolutely anything can be a work of art. The real problem, and this is Duchamp's great legacy to philosophy, is that we now need to work out a sufficient set of conditions for art. Several philosophers rose and are rising to this challenge, seeking to treat all manifestations of art – painting, sculpture, music, literature, performance and dance, in terms of a general theory of symbols, thus examining the language of art. So art is not dead but what does certainly seem to be dead are old fashioned philosophies of aesthetics.

Art requires our left brains and our right brains to talk to each other and so give meaning to experiences which lie beyond the grasp of reason. Exactly how this works and what its limits are, if any, poses philosophical problems of great relevance, importance and difficulty, whose solutions would bring a greater breadth and balance to our cultural life.

Chapter 27

Philosophical Aesthetics

Aestheticians are a fractured lot. A survey of the many thousands of papers and books published on aesthetics will confront people with a cacophony of ideas from philosophers who are described as Functionalists and Proceduralists or Institutionalists, even as Expressionalists or Representationalists, each earnestly seeking to offer the penultimate word on the question 'What is art?' We say penultimate because even philosophers recognise they are only human and subject to error. They offer their ideas that they may be extended and advanced by others of like mind. Nevertheless aesthetics was one simply defined as the exercise of taste and the appreciation of beauty.

Aesthetics, or aisthatikes in old Greek, for perception has been kneaded, twisted, turned, flailed and even slaughtered in an effort to cook up a theory that will account for all the many permutations of art that contemporary artists produce. Of course in order to maintain their personal theories some of the more traditional aestheticians merely deny that many of the oddities offered as art are examples of art. It seems that in such cases it is the artist who is at fault rather than the theory that attempts to explain art. No doubt there are many attempts to make new art forms that fail.

Happenings of the 1960s are an example but aestheticians can take no credit for their failures. The esoteric nature of most theories of art prevent them from being absorbed and understood by the art-going public, who on the whole have little interest in philosophy. Many merely desire a pleasant afternoon perusing the exhibitions in their local galleries. For some it is an opportunity to discover what it is everyone is talking about, but few are concerned with why such talk is taking place. Although many may hold a tacit theory about what counts as art, which they feel is sufficient to distinguish works of interest from works of no importance, they would not desire their theory to be publicly exposed and tested, and understandably so.

Though some may read the wisdom of art critics in newspapers and magazines or listen attentively to gallery tour guides, art appreciation still tends to be a private activity. The point is that it is not aestheticians, critics or tour guides that are most responsible for the longevity of our art works. Rather it is artists and their tacit opinions of the art-going public that ensure the endurance of art. Before institutional public exhibitions of art became commonplace, artists' studios were turned into galleries and were often visited by those who could not afford or did not desire to buy art. So does philosophical aesthetics really have a place or is it merely whistling in the dark alone and fearful of its irrelevance? Some vote for the latter and the argument of recent aestheticians strengthens this view. For example the notion of aesthetic experience is no longer seen as the product of disinterested attention allowing for an emotional response to a work of art.

An aesthetic experience is fundamentally cognitive. It entails understanding and the grasping of connections and the only reason it is described as aesthetic is because it is applied to art works. In other words an aesthetic experience is no different from any other contemplative experience. What is different from any other is the reward obtained. Sincere aestheticians continue with their studious search for the essence of aesthetics without realising. The subject is art and its works and it is to be the fundamentals of art making. We must look as if we wish to philosophically unpack the hard cases that tend to sink aestheticians. A philosophy of art must tell us what objects may be called art and why. The task of critics is to pick up where philosophy and philosophers leave off and tell us if the art object in question is worthy or not and why.

Aestheticians tend to confuse and merge the practice of philosophy with the practice of criticism and demonstrate their perspectives with exemplary cases that have had years of public certification rather than with controversial works. To be sure some aesthéticians have contrived convoluted theories in an attempt to include such works in their philosophy but the esoteric nature of their arguments makes them unintelligible to all but a patient few.

Chapter 28

Devotion

Despite what even many artists appear to believe, art is not, and should not be, merely a skill. It should actually be completely and utterly the language of our feelings, our frame of mind and indeed even our devotion. The relationship between art and devotion reveals an array of visual expressions of human feeling, belief and loyalty. These are complex categories that cross cultures and religions. Devotion can be expressed in figurative and abstract forms through patterns and calligraphy and in a vast array of media.

Art can express attachment to a person or loyalty to a cause, religious piety or belief. Art communicates different sentiments and beliefs and the range of artistic and visual narrative conventions that convey various manifestations of devotion. There is a range of meanings of the word devotion and it is useful in examining how art can express feelings and beliefs which help us to understand the diversity of practices used in the production of devotional and religious art from across temporal and cultural geographies.

We shall see how devotion in all its complications and complicities is depicted in art which shows how the images operate in the public and private realm and how they arouse our sentiments and feelings and how they tell stories. Approximately one quarter of the world population is Christian yet despite the global presence, Christianity remains closely identified with Western culture and there is no doubt it has been a substantial influence in the development of art in the West. The representation of devotion in Christian art is not straightforward as there are many varying conventions and rules according to different sects of the religion. Paintings which inspire devotion can make the viewer think deeply about faith and belief. They can inspire the viewer to feel love, fear or respect for Christianity. These images are ordained to stir one's affections, heart and devotion, for often one is stirred by sight, by reading, by hearing. The predominance of figurative art in Western Christian tradition has perhaps established a set of expectations of what we want to see in devotional art. However, this may desensitise us to the way in which art from other faiths inspires or represents devotion. The ability to believe is our outstanding quality and only art adequately translates it into reality. For some artists their art is their entire life.

Chapter 29

Christian Art

Two thousand years of Christianity have inspired some of the most important works of art known to humankind. They span not just time but also the world. Christian places of worship and contemplation were often embellished with multiple art forms, painted frescoes, stone and glass mosaics, wood carvings, stained glass and in a time of declining literacy these images served to instruct the minds of the ignorant. Then more portable forms of religious art appeared including paintings and free standing sculpture. Devotional objects, rosary beads, reliquaries protecting remnants of saints were made into works of art often by the foremost artists and artisans of the day.

Christian practices became focused on books. While the words remained important, after the advent of the printing press not having to copy each religious text by hand changed the nature of the art form. Informing all the forms of Christianity is the theme of death. The role of death is seminal in Christianity. The focus on the eternal soul led to sarcophagi movements, frescoes, sculptures and books.

The primacy of the gospels and the reality of death established the theological and iconographical foundation of Christian art but the noticed difference of other forms of Christianity gave rise to the variations on the underlying theme. Those variations led to the works of art emphasising aspects as different as the ideal of simplicity, personal devotion to God and even the end of the world. They also share in even the most simple and humble Christian artistic forms, reminding us that potentially there are as many variations in Christian art as there are individual beliefs and believers. The figural representations of Christian art belong to the Helenistic Jewish iconographic tradition and are probably the earliest Christian paintings. They show that early Christians had already tacitly decided that depictions of Christ were acceptable and did not violate the prohibition of graven images.

The meaning of what appears in such frescoes becomes clear when we remember what happened between them. The walls decorated with frescoes are the oldest painted representations of religion in the world. Stained glass was also adopted by Christian churches, Gothic Renaissance and Baroque soon followed. Scenes followed depicting life and miracles. Renaissance and Baroque paintings and sculpture filled basilicas. Most enduring impressions are poignant memories of tumultuous yet glorious parts of the nation embedded within huge stones and bricks that make a church. One of the most famous and decorated church is the Sagrada Familia and the most famous artist Anton Gaudi. Places of contemplation. Their art and artists give rise to contemplation far into the vast and inhospitable wilderness of biblical renown, it dawns upon the weary traveller and adventurer as a haven of peace and a hospitable refuge.

"The time is at hand when a devouring fire shall reduce to ashes all the buildings which you have beheld here both public and private. And while I am still able, that from the temporal goods which have been conferred upon me shall give some little portion for the gain of my soul. Let everyone make their contribution to holy matters which will become the symbol of national unity among all the branches of power and regular citizens. So sad, so free the days that are no more. I beseech you all to live always in this most holy life. Assist me and deliver me and protect me from enemies and make me an inheritor of blessed life eternal. Partake of the sacred mysteries according to traditions.

Anyone can stop for meditation and try to answer the most important question of all, 'What am I living for and what do I need to do to make my life right?' Simplicity in the construction, severity in the whole nobility without arrogance and majesty without ostentation. An absence of visual and functional distraction supports the goal of monastic life, a concentration to God. As one artist said, 'The purpose of Christian art is washing to dust the daily life of our souls'. It is a creative force and is the interior life of contemplation described finished when the creator has achieved his intention in it.

Chapter 30

The Sublime

Awe and sublimity involves a response to something larger than ourselves, a perception and a need for accommodation referring to how we make sense of and adjust to what we experience and although we sometimes use the words without much thought the sublime has a long philosophical history. The concepts of awe and sublime are more or less the same and we use the words interchangeably. Recent renewed interest in these two words gives a chance to test some of the philosophers' claims about them as well as to modify some of the theories. There is much on which the philosophical tradition and empirical research agree. The awe and sublime are the complex mixed feelings of intense satisfaction sensed before a striking or inspiring object, event or act. It includes the positive feeling of exaltation viewing an object, natural wonder or a marvel of architecture.

It is a mixed experience, a combination of satisfying and discomforting elements which nevertheless overall is a positive and pleasant, and perceivers want the experience to continue. We are all aware of the physiological changes associated with the awe and sublime: goosebumps, dropped jaw, raised eyebrows, widened eyes and a sense of time slowing down. Recent empirical research is much more than an updated version of the somewhat crude physiology once put forward. Research not only deepens our understanding of the human brain but also can help some longstanding philosophical theories about awe and the sublime.

The pleasure of the sublime philosophically was based on the recognition of one's own power of reason in the face of the power of what is perceived. The experience involves an explicit awareness of oneself. It is said that the person experiencing the sublime is orientated outwards toward the external world and the brain regions associated with self-awareness are deactivated not activated. It appears that the experience involves a sense of belonging to something bigger. However it was found that in terms of brain activity experiences of sublime and beauty differ fundamentally. Apparently the overall patterns of brain activity during the experience were different.

The main question concerning the sublime is why it is pleasant rather than painful. Philosophy has identified three main sources of pleasure, the expansion of the imagination, the belonging to a whole larger than ourselves and the rising above everyday affairs. It provides a release which feels good. The sublime has to do with going up to the limit or the edge of normal experience or even exceeding it and it is not uncommon to connect sublime to religion. Various types of sublimity can be distinguished by their trigger, a powerful God, a formidable object. It's a thread, with the strands woven together. The transcendent thread concerns the ineffable and unnameable while the imminent tends to focus on the emotion, the perceptual and of the imaginative play in the experience.

Philosophers think that awe and the sublime refer to life changing and transformative experience, one that alters perception and it could be that it has interesting and beneficial therapeutic applications. Either way it is regarded as a rich experience running parallel to beauty but still aesthetic and imaginative. Philosophy could profit from the empirical investigation, as establishing the best relationship between psychology and philosophy will doubtless continue to be an ongoing issue. This case shows that they can collaborate in a fruitful way and profit from each other's work.

Chapter 31

Negative Sublime

Does the sublime still exist in the 21st century? Or have we become desensitised to the very concept in a mediated world. A concept widely discussed by philosophers in recent years, its linguistic patterns and potency seems to have become diluted through misuse of the term, as sublime has been used increasingly to refer to something that is simply beautiful. But the sublime distinguished from beauty carries more with it, negative connotations of awe. Compared to the pleasure of the beautiful, the pleasure of the sublime is, so to speak, negative. It involves a recoil as if thinking came up against what precisely attracts it, but as we continue to endlessly colonise it, becoming more comfortable with images and spectacles, the sublime experience itself appears fragile. The sublime exists outside language, words fail.

These artistic presentations seek an idiom to articulate the impossible and the unpresentable. The concept of the non-presentability of the sublime refers to the imagination's capacity through reason's superiority to comprehend the magnitude of something empirically great or even infinite that would otherwise lie beyond comprehension. Because there is in our imagination a striving to advance to the infinitive, while in our own reason there lies a claim to absolute totality, the very inadequacy of our faculty for estimating the magnitude of the things in the sensible world wakens the feeling of a supersensitive faculty in us.

The source of the sublime is never an object or a painting but in our mental representation of the thing in itself which exists beyond experience. So this experience can be known in the intellect that is beyond pure sensation. We can say no more than that the object serves for the presentation of a sublimity that can be found in the mind, for what is properly sublime cannot be contained in any sensible form but concerns only ideas of abstract reason. This presents the paradox of the sublime that in our experience of the sublime we are able to experience the thing in itself as it exists independent of our experience.

In principle the gap separating the phenomenal empirical objects of experience from the thing in itself is insurmountable, that is no empirical object, no representation of it can adequately present the thing, but the sublime is an object in which we can experience this very impossibility, this permanent failure of the representation to reach after the thing. Thus by means of the very failure of representation we can have a presentiment of the true dimension of the thing. That is also why an object evoking in us the feeling of sublimity gives us simultaneous pleasure and displeasure. It gives us displeasure because of its inadequacy to the thing idea, but precisely through this inadequacy it gives us pleasure by indicating the time in comparable greatness of the thing surpassing every possible phenomenal empirical experience.

Nature for example wakens in us the feeling of the sublime where the aesthetic imagination is strained to its utmost, where all finite determinations dissolve themselves, the failure appears at its purest. Perhaps the sublime may be better located in a profound sense of the incomprehensibility in which the sublime generates through obscurity and ignorance. It is our ignorance of things that causes all our admiration and chiefly excites our passions. Because the sublime is a subjective experience it's difficult to argue whether or not it can exist in a given way. Nobody can be told what it is, we have to experience it for ourselves. Given that the sublime is a subjective experience, arguably it cannot be located in any one place. This suggests that we have not exhausted its potential yet.

Chapter 32

Seeing

Art is not what we see but what we make others see. What do we see when we look at art? The makers and viewers of art may see the same object differently and these interpretations become more diverse across time periods and cultures. We like to think of art as having meaning, significance and appeal to humankind through the ages. We attribute visual material with having a kind of autonomous existence that makes us see the world around us in new ways. Perhaps most importantly we enjoy looking at art for its own sake and can appreciate it independently of any knowledge of its content.

Wandering through an art gallery can be a very personal, aesthetically pleasing experience. It can make us feel good. The aim of art is to explore the ways in which we look at art and to think about what others might see when viewing the same object. Some common threads that bind together art from broad geography show that art from all periods operates similarly. These themes suggest how we can look simultaneously at works of art from across the world. These themes enable us to consider art and its various meanings. In this way we might be more aware from the kind of narratives where art from cultures outside the West is judged by Western standards. However, we see art as having added value because the works are produced self-consciously by the West to appeal to Western intellectual sensibilities.

The aim is to present a different view of how art relates to time and to think about how we encounter and experience art, how art is presented to us and what we bring to it as viewers. Perhaps the last word should be that a painting speaks for itself. What is the use of giving explanations when all is said and done. A painter has only one language. The artists yields often to the stimuli of materials that will transfer and transmit his spirit. When art dresses in worn out material it is most easily recognised as art. Artists find they can say things with colour and shapes they cannot say in any other way, things they have no words for.

Seeing and seeing as, are only part of the process of looking at an art work. Great art is the outward expression of an inner life in the artist and his inner life will result in his personal vision of the world. Art works can sometimes be strangely familiar. A work can appear to represent the world we know but there is something unreal about it too. Art does not reproduce the visible, rather it makes visible. We project our own impulses onto things we see and everyday objects lose their familiarity when reconfigured through this means of display, and special incongruities create a kind of cognitive dissonance. There are many ways of seeing art depending on your class or cultural viewpoint. It can make us think about ourselves in a certain way. It is the power of art and the art of power, through the aesthetics to look very carefully at the works themselves in order to make sense of them. Art is not solely about connoisseur values, that is the appreciation of what things look like, it moves art away from the importance of the aesthetic and helps us to disassociate the art work from both the artist and patron to see how it functions in its own right.

Chapter 33

Hidden Art

Looking at art, this may seem simple, but modern artistic theories have made this unnecessarily convoluted. Two ideas in particular, that art can exist for its own sake, as if anything can, and that everything and anything can be art, have so clouded the debate that art itself has become hidden. The cliché runs, 'I know what I like', but the truth is that you only have to look at art to know about it. The proof is in the looking. If a work of art does not speak to you, there is a strong chance it has actually nothing to say. So how do you recognise art? You know it when you see it, and seeing is everything.

Art lights up the place where it is, a wall, a room, all around you, and art glows in your mind when you look at it and it makes you more visually alert, more conscious and more alive. It's this uplifting mental light that we look for when hunting for art, the stimulus we get from looking at art, expressions of real feelings. The trouble is, for every artist who is genuinely inspired there are hundreds if not thousands of would-be artists who dress themselves up in artistic clothes. Of course few artists are on top form all the time, even great ones produce dull, lifeless work now and again.

The only way to sort out genuinely strong art from weak imitation is to look for it and trust our response. Much genuine art is hidden in every generation, often side-lined by the showy creations of shallow self-promoters and in our day by day bevy of con men and chancers. It is a long drawn-out process weeding out the art that is worth looking at and which everyone should get the chance to see, and that's what some have spent a lifetime doing in galleries, museums and other establishments, hunting for art that truly merits public display and which can have a lasting impact. They wanted to show real works of art to the public rather than droning on with slides in darkened rooms or for that matter writing art books that show illustrated glossy prints. This should be about looking at the art beyond the page. It involves handling art, lifting paintings, moving sculptures and sorting through prints, water colours and drawings, and also to know the back of pictures as well as their fronts, feel the weight of objects and become familiar with how they have been made.

We became intensely aware that art is the product of human hands as well as minds. Like seeing behind the scenes in a theatre makes the works of art more accessible and less mysterious, but at the same time our admiration grows for the artistry and imagination that went into their making. So began a lifetime of looking at real art in the locations the works were made for and where they still survived. We came increasingly to prefer art in its living context rather than the inevitably artificial and often regrettably precious atmosphere of museums and the like. Seeing real art is almost always surprising. First of all there is its scale. Most people glaze over when reading the height, weight and depth of an object, but even if they persevere and try to imagine it in their mind's eye, seeing it in three dimensional reality is a totally different experience. Then we don't have to calculate, all we do is feel. Our lives would be much depleted if great works of art were lost from sight.

There is a difference between an age when everything was handmade and our own era of impersonal mass production. One of the great strengths of visual art is that like music it can communicate directly across language barriers. The meaning of art from aft times and cultures can hit us suddenly like a lightening flash. It is only later if we can listen carefully that we can hear the boom that locates the source of the explosion. We have tried to use words to trace these sources of artistic inspiration to evoke some of the beliefs, thoughts and feelings that went into the making of the works of art, but I am painfully aware that words are clumsy when used to describe purely visual sensations. Verbal descriptions can never be more than an approximation of experiencing the real thing. All art worthy of the name is multi layered and this can only lift one or two veils on meanings that might at first be buried. It is only a beginning, a stimulus to further looking. The real art that it's about is hidden beyond it and much art has always been hidden but in different ways. The best art you have never seen could have been solely about obscure works of art. Public access to works of art is being restrained by the extortionate financial demands of these custodians and many places of art which in their ceaseless imperative to generate income have sadly compromised their educational remit.

The artist predominantly sees in the modern world increasingly what someone with a vested interest, usually a dealer, has paid us to see. Art works have all at some point, or in some way been hidden from view, but it is not solely about the hidden meaning of art that is not at first apparent and doesn't just illustrate neglected art that ought to be better known, instead it takes a broader view examining in what ways it's hidden today and asking whether it could make a greater contribution to our lives while, claiming to be custodians of art, nearly all places of art, museums, galleries bury countless treasures in storerooms, the worst being those that harbour loot from imperial times. This is a plea for the right to see the great art of the world. More than that it is a cri de coeur for the creation and showing of much better art today. If we feel more ambitious about what we would like to receive through our eyes we will have done our job. Looking at art is a way of making contact with people and an aid to a journey of discovery. We need to inspire further interest in art and challenge received opinion. Art transcends beliefs and time. Across the globe there are scores of beautiful and unusual works of art that are largely unseen or fail to receive the critical acclaim they deserve. Neglected wonders shut away in museums, storerooms, some hidden by chance, choice, to avoid destruction or for use in the afterlife.

Many are hidden by changes of taste, marginalised because they do not fit into the established norms of art. Other great works have been as good as hidden by the demands of conservation, and there are plenty of art treasures still to be revealed that have been hidden from view for some reason or another.

Chapter 34

The World Of Art

Everything we know about art is wrong. All artists are tortured geniuses who live bohemian but impoverished lifestyles. Art is a young person's game. Art is a useless waste of money. Primitive art is inferior to Western art. A true work of art must be unique. Between the ancient world and the Renaissance, art was effectively dead. Art is all about wandering around galleries. Women could not make a career out of art until the 20th century. True artists should do the work themselves. We all have a picture in our heads of the stereotypical artist, a tatterdemalion maestro frantically working at his canvas, a loner locked away in his garret for hours.

The artist must suffer for his art. Is all that right? Of course not. Artists come in all shapes and income brackets. What about the notion that mental instability can drive creativity? After all, creative people are by definition those who are able to use their minds in ways that others can't, and the old platitudes that there is a fine line between madness and genius might seem reasonable were found to be 25% more likely to, according to one study of artist and other creative professionals, carry genes that are associated with bipolar disorder and schizophrenia. To bend a crass cliché, you don't have to be crazy to work as an artist but it helps. It could be that those with mental illness are drawn towards the arts.

The passionate struggle may be seen in some artists but it is also true of anyone with a driven mind. It is also not true that art is a young person's game. Some of the greatest creative works in history came from the imaginations of people in their 60s and upwards. Art though history has many purposes other than to look pretty and that is still true today. Next time somebody blithely declares that art is useless and a waste of time, the following shows how useful art can be: as an aid to learning, for political propaganda, for devotion and meditation, to amuse, for therapy, as an investment, to show off, for diplomacy, to advertise, for local regeneration, and to relieve oneself. Primitive art comes from a culture that is closer to humanity's pre civilisation's existence.

Their creators can still astound. Primitive art, usually seen as inferior, now finds a prominent place in Western galleries. We like to think of creative works as unique but a surprising amount of art has more of one form of existence. A change sometimes levelled at medieval art is that it is all a bit samey. For centuries artists depicted well known biblical scenes in very similar styles with little innovation. This is a prejudice of the era we live in. It's natural to think that artists have always strived to be different, to create something original and to stand out from the crowd. This has not been the case especially among ancient civilisations. Artists more often worked within a strict set of customs and stylistic conventions. The art was not to produce beautiful original art but to carry on a tradition.

A trained eye can find different styles across territories and cultures, but that was nothing like the pace of change since the Renaissance. This does not imply that mediaeval artists and artistic traditions are inferior, only that they are different to those we have grown up with. We do not need to visit galleries to appreciate the artistic association between the two, which is strong. Art galleries are extremely popular and are always packed. There are many ways to see art outside of a gallery and there are many alternative ways of appreciating traditional arts without going to a gallery. It is harder to conjure up a list of famous female artists from earlier centuries. Women were largely discouraged from the paint brush. In many cultures some have traditionally been associated with the decorative arts and crafting, rather than the so-called fine arts like painting and sculpture.

As artists in their own right, a tour around any gallery of historical art will not yield much evidence, nor will a glance at the top auction sales. What about genuine female artists? The truth is that no period of artistic history has lacked female artistic talent. The division between fine arts and decorative arts is laden with historical snobbery. This is Western prejudice with its roots in the Renaissance. The decorative arts have enjoyed much higher status in other eras and other cultures. The 19th century brought greater access but still with restrictions. These decades saw a marked increase in the number of women who were able to exhibit works at academia and galleries.

Helpers and assistants to artists were engaged in menial, unskilled tasks but to some critics any assistance is too much assistance. It played havoc with our romantic notions of what an artist should be. The idea of a lone genius both conceiving and executing a masterpiece is infinitely more seductive than a group of anonymous hirelings working under the direction of an absent manager. Not all forms of art would be credible if left to an assistant. We would feel cheated if the moody, personal vision of the Impressionists turned out to be a team effort. Then too it would be wrong to assume all contemporary artists go down the route of hiring assistants.

Chapter 35

Portrait Painter

Lucien Freud remains one of our most influential artists, but he was more than just a painter of portraits. He was a philosopher too, wanting to glimpse the truth of the sitter before him, seeking to discover the real person by intimate observation. It has been pronounced that it is impossible nowadays for an advanced artist to paint a portrait, but there was one painter, Lucien Freud, who spent his entire long career doing nothing else. Indeed he expanded the notion of portraiture beyond its historical boundaries. As Freud interpreted it, the idiom of portrait was not just a depiction of a specific individual human being. Anything, absolutely anything, was, when he painted it, an example of portraiture.

He once insisted that even two exact examples of a manufactured article would prove on close examination to be slightly different. Every single thing that an artist's eye might encounter was individual and what you might call the individuality of individuals was his true subject, their faces, their bodies, their personalities and their moods. Moreover he was interested, he often said a bit surprisingly, in the effect his sitter had on the space and objects around them. The background of the painting was all about what the head was doing to it.

Perhaps the best way of understanding this without subscribing to a belief in extra sensory perception is that he was highly sensitive to the way that each sitter affected him. Each made the things have a distinct presence and particular physical and emotional output. Each made the things round about him look a bit different to him. Thus each portrait was the product not only of the individuality of the subject but also of the personality of the artist. It was something unique by someone unique. He was once asked what he was thinking about when he painted a portrait. His answer was 'The anatomy of the individual'. So he wasn't trying to depict an unusual body but a particular person with characteristics not quite like anyone else's.

The only common factor in his subjects, vastly varied in age, gender and physique and ranging from criminals and bohemians to the Queen, is that none of them were nondescript. Right from the beginning he was a very slow painter. A portrait head might take the 150 hours other painters calculated that was required, but he would take equivalently longer.

This estimate refers only to the formal sitting in the studio, the period for which he was actually painting and the sitter posing. In addition there were hours spent conversing. To a sitter who once asked if he could speed up, he replied 'I can only work in my own time'. That luxurious prolongation of the process was not an eccentricity but was essential because the whole point of the procedure was to see more.

That is to gather the maximum amount of information about his sitter. He was highly conscious of how much people changed from day to day, even from hour to hour. It wasn't just the posing, it was from the mind, and vitalities fluctuated as did the painter's too. So the longer he looked at his sitter the more was revealed. In his early work there is an enormous amount of detail. Each fleck in the irises of his sitter's eyes, each hair seems to have been scrutinised as if he had examined them from very close. His paintings are always intimate and, a word he liked, private. Later on his painting techniques became looser and broader, his paintings came to include an amazing quality of information about skin, texture and the forms of the face.

He was always on the lookout for such things. After nearly a year of sitting he noticed even a little fold under, say, the chin. Immediately this went into etchings he was doing. The little form helped, he said, meaning that it improved the architecture and shapes and textures. In the end he often said that art was about the life forms. According to his personal rules, all of those he used in his paintings had to be discovered in the sitter, the person he was looking at. His conception of art was in its way as radical, even as subversive, as Greenberg's modernist manifesto. According to the latter, there was no more interest for a painter in the appearance of the world and its inhabitants. The implication was that photographs could deal with all that.

There were no fresh discoveries to be made in figurative art with paint and brushes. Instead artists would explore shapes, line and colour for their own sake, what is known as abstraction. These ideas were already current when Freud was a young painter. Nevertheless he began to work in a completely contrary manner and carried on resolutely doing so while in fashion and out for his whole life. Everything in his paintings is the opposite of abstract, concrete, awkward, factual and nothing even idealistic or generalised. European art inherited a notion of the human body from the ancient Greeks defined as the nude.

It is heroic, harmonious and not much like any actual human being. Freud's people were the reverse, naked, poor, bare, forked creatures which some find shocking and ugly because they are so clearly of real exposed people, but the more you look at them, it is believed, the richer and in a way the more human they become.

He once said that he had only one secret, conversation and concentration, and you cannot teach that. He had another, so people thought, he was immensely and unendingly interested in people. Everyone who met him was immediately fascinated. He was thin, wore very well tailored, well worn clothes. He took a long while setting things up. The one unusual thing was that he answered the phone if it rang. Because he worked slowly he could talk and he would look intensely for a while, his eyes very piercing and rarely lowered. Then he mixed as he would talk. His palette was of light colours and he never cleaned it, just smoothed out bits for mixing for every change of tone.

His paintings are remarkable works by a great artist who rarely travelled and rarely left London. He was sociable and liked restaurants and a smoke-free atmosphere. He was a painter who said the only way he could work properly was using absolute maximum observation and maximum concentration. He thought that by staring at his sitter and subject matter and examining it closely he could get something from it. He had a lot of eye trouble and terrible headaches because of the strain of painting so close.

Chapter 36

Angles On Art

Philosophy askes why we judge certain things to be beautiful and whether we can apply this judgement to the appreciation of art. This includes the Western understanding of art up until the 20th century as being primarily about beauty, but by then the paradigm for art was that anything counts. An art work does not even have to be a thing. It can be flashing lights in a room, stacked up papers, a pile of vomit or someone running around a gallery, anything in fact.

Since art is a purely humanly constructed idea, it is not a natural kind of thing, so this allows that ultimately art is whatever we mean by it, so the art question becomes, on what basis do we give the word art one meaning rather than another? Nowadays presenting anything in a gallery is enough to make it art, for the contemporary understanding is that art is whatever the artist designates his art to be. Along with this shift in what art is, came a shift in the idea of what art is for. Before the 20th century the purpose of art was considered to be to please the senses and refine the sensibilities. Now most seem to consider its purpose to be to stimulate new ways of viewing the world.

By presenting things in a novel way like everyday objects in galleries is only one approach, the viewer is provoked to see things from new angles and so gain new ways of seeing. Like all cultural moments this shift in perspective on art itself is but a step in the history of thought. Indeed only one reason that art is valuable for society is that it is often at the spearhead of a culture's evolving thoughts and attitudes. Even now there is a shift back towards individualistic emotional expression. This suggests that the new art culture will come to be seen as pluralist. If modernism can be summarised as the rejection of all values perhaps pluralism can be defined as the acceptance of all values.

All art works display some of their artist's creative values and we should value them for this. Wherever we go from here, art has broken free of the gilded age of formal beauty and this has opened up the creative horizon. The post-modern shift in the ideals of art away from prescribed values has indeed resulted in an explosion of artistic possibilities and without a doubt many new ways of doing art have delivered many wonderful creations that would have seemed otherwise inconceivable before. However, the side-lining of values of beauty and technical skill undoubtedly also means that something precious has been lost.

The art world confronts two questions, what is to be deemed art, and who decides? But it did not overthrow the art world's power of art establishment, rather our cultural arbiters of artistic value reacted by adopting the somewhat meaningless view that anything and everything is art. Consequently for theoretical critics, for a work of art to be admired has become not about its splendour nor the fineness of its construction, but the cleverness of its concept within art culture, whilst the practical criteria for judging one work better than another seems to be the fame of the artist and the price it fetches in the market. Yet surely there is something wrong with the art world if a work of art is not to be judged by its quality, but simply by the cleverness of its concept.

So although it seems the answer to the question, what is art, has been won by in this epoch anything that someone in the art world community calls art, the question of whether a particular art work is any good is not settled by the opinions of curators and critics but through the mastery, and the opinion, of the high end market. Instead whether a work of art is good as art is a question to be decided by individuals for whatever reason and whatever criteria we will wish to use for our judgement including many diverse ideals of beauty and skill. However much it will be able to be sold for is really beside the point.

Chapter 37

Clarifying Terms

Art is a skill applied to design, representation and imaginative creation. It is a human skill as opposed to nature. It is also a cunning stratagem and a subject in which skill may be exercised in certain branches of learning traditionally serving as preparation for more advanced study to obtain a standard of proficiency concerned with the design and decoration of objects for practical use, i.e. handicrafts, or of fine arts, painting, sculpture, architecture, music, literature and poetry, carrying out performance art exacting notable feats, and performing plays for public exhibition. Poetry is the art work of the poet who expresses beautiful or elevated thoughts, imagination of feeling in appropriate language and use in metrical form.

Poems showcase quality in anything that calls for practical poetical expression and prose which has all the qualities of poetry except metre. The painter paints pictures of works of art executed with attention to light, shade, mass, tone and form rather than life. So what is the medium of paint? It is a solid colouring matter suspended in a liquid vehicle used to impart colour to a surface, something especially medicament put on like paint with a brush. Sculpture on the other hand is the art of forming representations of objects in the round or in relief by chiselling stone, carving wood, modelling clay, casting metal or similar processes.

Then we come to beauty which has a combination of qualities as a form and colour that delights the eye and other senses, the moral sense or the mind. A beautiful trait or feature, a person or thing possessing beauty agreeable to mind, feelings and senses. It feeds our perceptions, our intuitive recognition in which our mind refers its sensations to external objects and art. Literature is an art form of literary production in the literary profession. Writings whose value lies in beauty of form and emotional effort and effect. All art uses imagination, the mental faculty forming images of external objects not present to the senses such as fancy, it's a creative faculty of the mind.

Art improves and refines the mind by education and also intellectual development. Aesthetics, philosophy of the beautiful and philosophy of art appreciation of the beautiful, having such appreciation in accordance with principles of good taste. Sublime transmutes into a state more refined, regarded as higher in cultural or moral scale of the most exalted kind and far above the ordinary, inspiring awe, deep reverence, lofty emotion by beauty, vastness or grandeur which elevates and purifies. It's also below the threshold of consciousness too faint or rapid to be recognised and which affects behaviour.

Seeing is to perceive by sight and mentally ascertain by doing so. It's having the power to discern objects. Perspective is the art of delineating solid objects on a plane surface so as to give the same impression of relative position, magnitude as the objects do when viewed from a particular point, pictures so painted or drawn with apparent relation in which parts of the subject are viewed by the mind. Conceptualism is a doctrine that universals have, reality but only as mental concepts. Psychological doctrine that the mind is capable of forming ideas corresponding to abstract and general terms.

Chapter 38

Conclusion

To summarise, this book endeavoured to answer three questions:

What is art?

What does art do?

What is art for?

Art is an artist made skill which is born from each individual artist's creative concepts, ideas and imagination. It is an illusion of image, nowadays dominated by technology, which can distant, alter, add and take away from the originals represented. It is a communication of artistic concepts which define humanity, the language which provokes feelings, awareness, spirituality and thoughts and senses. Today it has become anything anyone deems it to be. It is culturally dependent. Art answers the artist's desire and passion to create and the philosopher's to debate and discuss the philosophical aspects of art. In its various forms it enables people to shape their own ideas and perceptions of what is being viewed. It is also of our time as it drives our development, forcing changes, so creating cultural movement. It links society and humanity, bringing people together.

Art supports establishment and also engenders tolerance and respect. It is for all and has something for everyone. Art today is considered to be to produce art in new ways, its purpose to make its audience respond, provoked into seeing what's before them in different ways and by different angles. With art today being readily available for everyone, artists now produce art to arouse and stimulate and engage us all, for us to perceive both the art and ourselves in a different way and our world in total. It challenges us in order to see things from a new perspective. It has a valuable purpose for society because it is the pinnacle of culture's evolving thoughts which opens up creative horizons.

Note

The world needs art, artists and philosophers.

www.ingramcontent.com/pod-product-compliance
Ingram Content Group UK Ltd.
Pitfield, Milton Keynes, MK11 3LW, UK
UKHW040031200726
13854UKWH00001B/466